ALASKA HISTORY NO. 38

MAPS OF RUSSIAN AMERICA
II

THE LOVTSOV ATLAS
of the
North Pacific Ocean

Compiled at Bol'sheretsk, Kamchatka, in 1782
from discoveries made by Russian mariners and
Captain James Cook and his officers

by
Vasilii Fedorovich Lovtsov

Translated, with an Introduction and Notes
by
Lydia T. Black

Edited by
Richard A. Pierce

THE LIMESTONE PRESS

Kingston, Ontario : Fairbanks, Alaska

1991

P.O. Box 1604
Kingston, Ontario
Canada K7L 5C8

U.S. Office:
The Limestone Press
c/o History Department
University of Alaska, Fairbanks
Fairbanks, Alaska 99775-0860

International Standard Book Number 0-919642-38-1

Publication was funded in part by the Alaska Humanities Forum, Anchorage, and the National Endowment for the Humanities.

Production: Pauline Higdon

Printed and bound in Canada by: Brown & Martin Limited
Kingston, Ontario

CONTENTS

INTRODUCTION

Until recently, the Russian contribution to the cartography of the North Pacific Ocean was either ignored in western literature (Wagner 1937) or mentioned only tangentially (Friis, editor 1967). The few authors who are aware of the significant work done in this region by Russian navigators (Gibson, Falk) follow, in the main, the lead of Russian and Soviet historians of cartography (Bagrow, Shibanov, Medushevskaia, and Efimov, to mention but a few), and their work, though valuable is by necessity not complete: the great wealth of archival cartographic materials in Soviet archival depositories itself defeats a complete study.

Just how incomplete these studies are is evidenced by the fact that the name of an important 18th century cartographer, Navigator Lovtsov, does not appear at all in many major publications on the subject (Bagrow 1975, Medushevskaia 1975, Shibanov 1975). Thus, the discovery in the Provincial Archives of British Columbia at Victoria of a handpainted atlas by Navigator Lovtsov is an exciting event.

The Provincial Archives acquired the Lovtsov Atlas from a used book dealer in Leipzig, Germany for 1200 Marks. A library stamp on one of the pages of the atlas (in Latin) indicates that it was originally part of a gymnasium library, possibly in Irkutsk. Nothing else is known about the history of the atlas.

The atlas itself is a hand-bound book, in hard cover, of folio sheets, 27.5 x 20.5 inches. A number of pages are blank. Eighteen charts, two of which cover two facing pages, are executed in pen and water colors. Each chart as a rule carries at least one cartouche or medallion within which the author provides information on the sources of the chart or charts.

Before I discuss each individual chart in the atlas, I should like to state what is known of Lovtsov himself and his service in the North Pacific. Unfortunately, the information is scant and had to be pieced together on the basis of tangential remarks contained in documents which address a variety of topics, from the Krenitsyn/Levashev Expedition of 1767-1768 to Alaska, to Adam Laxman's embassy to Japan (1792-1793).

If we can credit two paraphrases of Laxman's report, Lovtsov told Japanese officials in the spring of 1793 that he had sailed in the Pacific seas for 32 years. He therefore (Anon. 1805:73) must have arrived for service in Okhotsk about 1761 (Polonskii 1871:508). If so, he may have been one of the three navigators assigned in 1761 to the port of Okhotsk or one of eleven apprentice navigators assigned there in 1760 (Sgibnev 1869:44). He may have been a graduate of either the Nerchinsk Navigational School or the Irkutsk Navigational School. The former was opened in 1755 by F. I. Soimonov, and merged with the latter in 1765 (Kopylov 1974:72-73), but this is conjecture only.

That Lovtsov was an apprentice navigator when he arrived in Okhotsk is indicated by the fact that he is so listed in a document relating to the Levashev/Krenitsyn Expedition: In 1767, Apprentice Navigator Vasilii Lovtsov was dispatched from Bol'sheretsk to Tobol'sk with papers from Krenitsyn and was to report to the governor. Interestingly, Lovtsov was detained, 6 April by Col. Plenisner in Okhotsk and the packet he was carrying was opened. (See Divin, editor 1979:350, Sgibnev 1869:49). Krenitsyn filed a protest with the Admiralty (Narochnitskii, 1989:358-359, note 63). In the years that followed it appears that Lovtsov was regularly taking crown vessels from Okhotsk on the Kamchatka run (Alekseev 1958:81), and, in fact is known to have made two runs in a single season, a remarkable feat for the time. By 1789, Navigator Lovtsov, serving in Okhotsk as Post Pilot, held the rank of Lieutenant, Junior Grade [praporshchik].

On 8 September 1789 Lovtsov was in charge when the ship <u>Dobroe Namerenie</u>, newly built for the Billings Expedition, was being towed to sea. A squall came up, and the vessel was lost. However, Billings, an Englishman in Russian navy service, reporting the accident, characterized Lovtsov as a very experienced officer (Billings, 12 Sept 1789, in Divin, editor, 1979:378-379). The maritime historian Sgibnev, who rarely had a good word to say about the Far Eastern navigators, be they merchantmen, skippers or graduates of the provincial navigational schools, had nothing but high praise for Lovtsov, who, according to Sgibnev, had until then never lost a ship (1869). Sgibnev said that Lovtsov served in Okhotsk for forty years and died there (Sgibnev, 1869). However, on 10 August 1795, the Ruling Senate ordered that Vasilii Fedorovich Lovtsov, who formerly held the rank of <u>praporshchik</u> be elevated to the rank of <u>poruchik</u> and be permitted, in recognition of his services, to retire with full pay (Polonskii 1871:541).

That Lovtsov, indeed, was held to be a responsible, experienced, and good navigator is clear from the role he was assigned in the Adam Laxman expedition (or, as some call it, embassy) to Japan. While Laxman had the responsibility for trade negotiations with the Japanese, Lovtsov was given full responsibility for outfitting the vessel and the conduct of marine operations (Narochnitskii, 1989:316-320, Document No. 117). In fact, he acted in concert with Laxman throughout the expedition which lasted from the fall of 1792 to 8 September 1793 and co-signed letters to the Japanese authorities (Narochnitskii, 1989:312-313, Documents 112 and 113). Lovtsov submitted at least two joint reports with Laxman to the Russian government, and a special separate report on 18 January 1794 (Polonskii, 1871). He submitted a journal and two charts (Narochnitskii, 1898:316, Document No. 117, note 96 p.364, and Alekseev, 1987:138). Lovtsov was, together with Laxman, received by Empress Catherine the Great 13 June 1794 at Tsarskoe Selo (Divin 1971:319). Ivan Pil, reporting to Empress Catherine on the outcome of the expedition to Japan had the following to say: "Finally, I cannot remain silent before the sacred throne of Your Imperial Majesty about [the role of] participants in the said expedition.

Navigator Lieutenant Junior Grade [praporschik] Lovtsov and Lieutenant [poruchik] Laksman. The first mentioned, as part of his long term naval duty here in Okhotsk, in the course of which he voyaged to various destinations in the local waters, completed the voyage to Japan, hitherto a destination unknown to him, in a manner wished for..." (Narochnitskii, 1989:320).

Lovtsov's ability as a cartographer is evident from the description of his interactions with Japanese who copied his maps and also copied Japanese maps for him (Polonskii 1871). One American scholar states that Russian charts of Japan, left there by the Laxman expedition in 1792-1793, affected the development of Japanese cartography (Lensen 1954:7). Lovtsov charted the harbor of Nemuro on Hokkaido in 1792, Matsumae and Hakodate. That Lovtsov's mission to Japan was well known to the officers of the Russian navy is attested by the fact that V. M. Golovnin named the strait between the Kurile islands of Iturup and Kunashir in 1811 for Lovtsov's vessel (the Ekaterina proliv Ekateriny (Lupach, editor 1953:524, 590).

This atlas, then, represents a new datum to be added to our understanding of Russian cartography in the North Pacific. It demonstrates not so much the state of the art in the last quarter of the 18th century, as the fact that Russian cartographers tried to keep abreast of geographic information being developed by the rival powers and that the Russian navigators in Okhotsk and Kamchatka had at their disposal a collection of European maps which they respected, copied, checked, verified or disproved, and, when needed, corrected.

ACKNOWLEDGEMENTS

In nearly a decade I spent on researching the provenance of the Atlas of Navigator Lovtsov and his biography, several individuals freely rendered their expert help when I needed it. Without it, this book would never have written.

I should like to acknowledge, first of all, the assistance of Commander A.C.F. David (RN ret.), an authority on the cartography of Cook's voyages of discovery. He provided me with photos of the chart of Petropavlovsk Harbor from Roinberts' manuscript journal and was instrumental in obtaining copies of charts possibly drawn by members of Cook's Third Voyage, now in the Naval Archives of the USSR. His analysis of photographs of charts by Lovtsov, allegedly based on material supplied the Russians in 1779 by Cook's officers, helped me immeasurably. Dr. Richard Pierce, who first came upon the atlas, urged me to undertake this study. Dr. Marvin Falk, Curator, Rare Books, Rasmuson Library of the University of Alaska Fairbanks, an authority on cartography of the North Pacific basin, supplied me with a listing of all published charts from Cook's voyage, as well as the listing of locations of manuscript charts and all possible English language publications on Russian cartography. He also introduced me to Commander David. Mr. J. MacIntosh, Curator of Rare Books and Maps at the Library of the University of British Columbia, travelled from Vancouver to Galiano Island to personally deliver to me excellent copies of charts and maps of Japan published in the Teleki Atlas and thus enabled me to establish the provenance of Lovtsov's map of Honshu Island.

Last, but by no means least, I should like to thank the staff of the Map Section, in particular, David R. Chambairlain, Head, Library and Map Section, Province of British Columbia Archives, for unfailing courtesy and assistance during my several visits and for putting at my disposal color slides and black-and-white photographs of the Lovtsov Atlas.

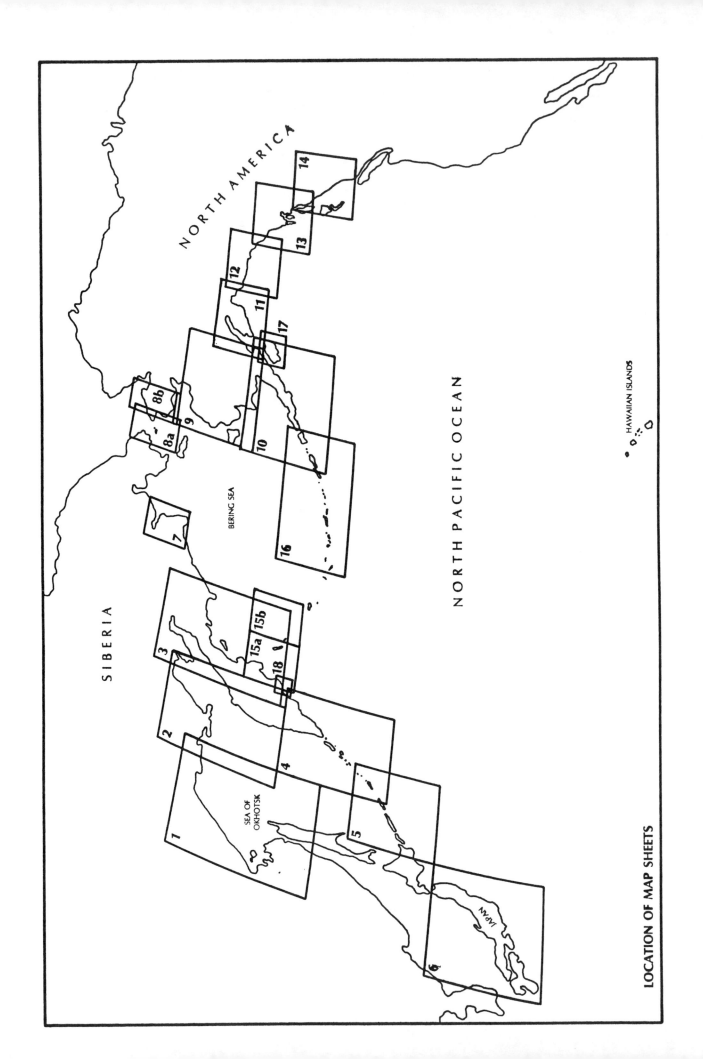

LOCATION OF **MAP SHEETS**

THE ATLAS

This volume is the only compendium of charts known to have been drawn by Lovtsov. It contains the following charts, with lists of place names. Some of the terms are still in use, others are recognizable but altered, and some have been replaced by others; many were difficult to read, so certain renditions are only approximate. Many of the terms would be of interest of analyzed from a linguistic standpoint, but that could not be undertaken here.

<u>Legends on the Title Page:</u>

a) Inscription within the cartouche in the center of the page:

"A T L A S
by Navigator Lovtsov composed by him
while wintering at the Bol'sheretsk ostrog
in the year 1782"

b) Inscription within the cartouche at the top of the page:

"COMPILED FROM VARIOUS DESCRIPTIONS

by gentlemen of the Okhotsk Port and officers of the previous [naval] expedition, and drawn in the Mercator projection, [the coast] from the Uda to the port of Okhotsk and E to Taunskaia [guba] and from the latter to the N, to the lama, Gizhiga and Penzhina inlets; the coast to the southern cape [extremity] of Kamchatka called the Kuril'skaia Lopatka, encompassing the rivers which empty into the sea; and also maps of the Kurile Islands, the Aleutian Islands, and a map of Japan.

"[The area] from Lopatka northward, to Petropavlovskaia Harbor, together with the rivers which empty into the sea, and from the Harbor to Karaginskii Island, and from the latter to the mouth of the Anadyr' and along the Anadyr' River upstream [is based] on the declarations of service men who frequent these regions, confirmed in the their exactness by declarations given here by [officers of] the two English ships under command of Mr. Commodore Cook, his captains, Messrs. Clerke and Gore. Their notes, translated here by the former Kamchatka Commander von Behm, were [the basis for] the chart of Chukotskii Nos up the line to the north indicating the limit [of their voyage]. Regions which were not investigated, and the reasons therefore, are [also] indicated in the atlas."

1

CHART 1

The coast of the Sea of Okhotsk, from 55° N lat. NE to 59°15' N lat., with the Shantar Islands and the Island of Sakhalin. This chart is of interest in that it clearly demonstrates Russian knowledge of Sakhalin as an island by 1782 and probably much earlier.

A. <u>Sakhalin Island</u>, with a total of 8 streams [rivers] indicated, two debouching to the north, three to the east, and three to the west. Of these the following streams are named:

    1. River flowing to E. (southernmost indicated stream): Kudusi [var. Nudusi?]

    2. River flowing to W. (southernmost indicated stream): Chula [var. ?]

    3. River flowing to E. (northernmost indicated stream): Sai [Say] Sula.

B. <u>Islands off the Okhotsk shore</u>:

    4. Kurilskoi [island]

    5. Ostrov Shantar [Shantar Island]

    6. Goloi

    7. Goloi

    8. Feklisov

    9. Medvezhei

    10. Kronshlat

C. <u>Okhotsk Sea shore, South to North</u>:

    11. R. Porom (River Porom)

    12. R. Ud' (River Ud' or Uda)

    13. Armat' [Armat River]

    14. R. Aldama [Aldama River]

    15. R. Ul'ia [Ul'ia River]

Chart 1

16. R. Urak [Urak River]

17. R. Okhota [Okhota River]

18. R. Kukhtun [Kukhtun River]

19. Marikanka [Marikanka River]

20. M. Marikanskoi [Cape Marikanskii]

21. Ul'veia [Ul'keia River]

22. Ina [Ina or In'ia River]

23. Uliunza [River]

24. Shil'kapka [River]

25. M. Shil'kap [Cape Shil'kap]

26. Shil'kapskoi [Headland]

27. M. Girileiskoi [Cape Girileiskoi]

28. R. Temliachik [Temliachik River]

29. M. Temliachinskoi [Cape Temliachinskoi]

30. M. Melenkol' [Cape Melenkol'].

CHART 2

This chart, on two folio pages, shows the coast of the Sea of Okhotsk from ca. 59°15' N lat. to ca. 63° N lat. and the neck of the Kamchatka Peninsula, both the Okhotsk and Pacific shores. Eighty-six place names are given. Several active volcanoes are indicated. There is some overlap between Chart 2 and Chart 3.

1. M. Dyrand [Cape Dyrand]

2. Nerpich'ia [Nerpich'ia River]

3. Omokhton [River]

4. M. Motyklenskoi [Cape Motyklenskoi]

5. O. Korobei [Korobei Island]

6. O. Shalan talan [Shalan talan Island]

7. G. Motyklenskaia [Motyklenskaia Inlet, Guba]

8. R. Motyklen [River Motyklen]

9. G. Taunskaia [Guba -inlet- Taunskaia]

10. R. Taui [River Taui or Taun]

11. R. Iana [River Iana]

12. R. Arman' [River Arman']

13. G. Ol'skaia [Guba -inlet- Ol'skaia]

14. R. Ola [River Ola]

15. G. Opokina [Guba -inlet- Opokina]

16. O. Ol'skoi [Ol'skoi Island]

17. M. Alevin [Cape Alevin]

18. M. Bligan [Cape Bligan]

19. M. Vanvan [Cape Vanvan

20. M. Kinarchi [Knnarchi, Cape]

4

Chart 2

21. R. Siglan [Siglan River]

22. M. Maguis [Cape Maguis]

23. R. Lykich' [Lykich' River]

24. M. Al'kaibuliga [Al'vaibuliga Cape]

25. M. Apokhochin [Apokhochin Cape]

26. M. Piagin [Cape Piagin, var. Pniagin]

27. Baran [Baran Island]

28. Atykan [Atykan Island]

29. Motykil' [Motykil' Island]

30. Kakhoitse [var. Kakhontse, island]

31. G. Iama [Iama Inlet]

32. R. Iama [Iama River]

33. M. Iapon [Cape Iapon]

34. M. Malenei [Cape Malenei]

35. M. Iret' [Cape Iret']

36. R. Iret' [Iret' River]

37. R. Ant [Ant River]

38. R. Aregicha [Aregicha River]

39. R. Iovana [Iovana River]

40. R. Tumana [Tumana River]

41. M. Tumanskoi [Cape Tumanskoi]

42. R. Kananega [Kananega River]

43. R. Lakhtamina [Lakhtamina River]

44. M. Viliginskoi [Cape Viliginskoi]

Chart 2

45. R. Vilega [Vilega River]

46. R. Alevaia [Alevaia River]

47. R. Tovatoma [Tovatoma River]

48. R. Ul'kana [Ul'kana River]

49. R. Naiakhona [Naiakhona River]

50. M. Naiakhonskoi [Cape Naiakhonskoi]

51. G. Varkhalamska [sic, Varkhalamskaia Guba or inlet]

52. R. Varkhalam [Varkhalam River] - here begins overlap with Chart 3

53. M. Varakhalamskoi [Cape Varkhalamskoi]

The following place names appear on the shore of the Kamchatka Peninsula, N to S along the Okhotsk Sea coast, Nos. 54-77, No. 78 designating Kamchatka River, and Nos. 79-86 on the Pacific shore of the "neck" of the Kamchatka Peninsula.

54. M. Kuiul' [Cape Kuiul']

55. M. Cheiachegin [Cape Cheiachegin]

56. M. Mentelai [Cape Mentlai]

57. Tel'lan [name designates an offshore island or possibly a cape]

8. Getologo [sic, River]

59. M. Getologon [Cape Getologon]

60. M. Gallant [Cape Gallant]

61. R. Amanina [Amanina River]

62. Tigil' [River]

63. M. Amgon [Cape Amgon]

64. R. Kuvachina [Kuvachina River]

65. Utkholoka [River]

Chart 2

66. R. Kavran [River Kavran]

67. R. Khar'iuzova [Khar'uzova River]

68. R. Belogolova [River]

69. R. Morosheshna [River]

70. R. Soposhna [River]

71. R. Icha [River]

72. R. Oblukovina [River]

73. R. Krutogorova [River]

74. Myshkuian [River]

75. R. Kompakova [River]

76. R. Vorovska [sic, river]

77. R. Kol [River]

78. R. Kamchatka [Kamchatka River]

79. M. Chazhmiskoi [Cape Chazhmiskoi]

80. R. Chazhma [Chazhma River]

81. M. Kronots [sic, Kronotskoi Cape]

82. R. Stolbova [River]

83. Stolbovoi [sic, Cape S.]

84. Kronok [River or/and Lake]

85. R. Kamyshka [River]

86. R. Shemiachik

CHART 3

This chart, which overlaps slightly with Chart 2, focuses on the north coasts of the kamchatka Peninsula, both the Okhotsk and Pacific sides, with 79 place names indicated. It covers the coasts from Inzhiga [Izhiga] Bay to Penzhina Bay and the "neck" of Kamchatka Peninsula on Okhotsk and Pacific sides.

1. R. Varkhalam [River]

2. R. Inzhiga [sic, Inzhiga -or Izhiga River]

3. R. Ovekova

NOTE: A church is indicated off the right bank of the Izhiga River and an outpost on the sea shore between the mouths of the Izhiga and Obvekova Rivers.

4. Guba Inzhigi [Inzhiga Inlet or Inzhiginskaia Guba]

5. Chaibukun [? Island]

6. Matuga [Island]

7. Kuiul' [Cape]

8. R. Kangalega [River]

9. M. Cheiachegin [Cape]

10. R. Ukiten [var. Ukitei, River]

11. Menteli [sic, Cape]

12. Tel'lan [Island or headland at the mouth of the Ukiten River]

13. M. Tangonoskoi [Cape]

14. M. Povorotnoi [Cape]

15. Echegen' [locality or rover]

16. M. Pekula [Cape]

17. R. Serditaia [River]

18. R. Khalingancha [River]

Chart 3

19. R. Gorelaia [River]

20. R. Studenaia [River]

21. R. Kil'teeva [River]

22. Ostrova Kilteevskiia [Kil'teevskie Islands, a chain of 6]

23. M. Unkane [Ubnkane Headland]

24. M. Nechegat [Cape]

25. O. Pontelen [Island]

26. M. Kuiul' [Cape]

27. R. Egacha [River, at head of Penzhina Inlet]

28. Egachinskoi [Island]

29. Varganov [Island]

30. R. Zhirova [River]

31. M. Malchan [Cape]

32. M. Valaegen' [Cape]

33. R. Ekina [River]

34. R. Pustaia [River]

35. Mameta [River]

36. Goloi [Island]

37. Tannicha [Island]

38. Kannegaran [Island]

39. M. Itaigan [Cape]

40. R. Podkagarna [River]

41. R. Shemanka [River]

42. R. Lesnaia [River]

Chart 3

43. R. Tinkil' [River]

44. R. Pallan [River]

45. R. Bratov [River]

46. R. Kakhtana [River]

47. R. Urga [River]

48. R. Voianpolka [var. Koianpolka, River]

49. R. Geotologon [River]

50. M. Getologon [Cape]

51. M. Gamatyn [Cape]

52. R. Amanina [River, cf. Chart 2]

NOTE: Nos. 53 and following refer to the Pacific shore, S to N.

53. O. Stolbovskoe [Stolbovskoe Lake]

54. M. Kurant [Note: two capes are designated by this name, see below No. 57)

55. M. Ozernovskoi [Cape]

56. Ozerna [River, flowing out of a lake]

57. M. Kurant [Cape, cf. No. 54]

58. M. Ukinskoi [Cape]

59. Uka [River]

60. Bandara [River]

61. Kholiuli [var. Kholiuln, river]

62. M. Karaginskoi [Cape Karaginskoi]

63. Ostrov Karaginskoi [Karaginskoi Island]

64. R. Karaga [Karaga River]

65. Tyshakhapka [River]

Chart 3

66. G. Nerpich'ia [Nerpich'ia Inlet]

67. Napirka [River]

68. G. Napirka [Napirka Bay]

69. G. Koriatska [Koriatska --Koriak-- Bay]

70. Lilban [River, var. Anaban?]

71. G. Anapkova [Bay or Inlet]

72. O. Verkhoturskoi [Verkhoturskoi Island]

73. M. Gavanskoi [Cape]

74. Govenka [River]

75. Anabkova [River]

76. Alitora [River]

77. G. Aliutora [Aliutora Inlet or Aliutorskaia Bay]

78. M. Aliutorskii [Cape]

79. R. Pakhacha

CHART 4

This chart shows the southern part of the Kamchatka Peninsula, including Cape Lopatka, and the Northern Kurile Islands, from the first island through the north shore of the 16th, with 66 place names. The numbering proceeds from N to S along the Okhotsk Sea shore, turning from S to N along the Pacific shore (Nos. 23-49), and then to the Kurile Islands from N to S. There is some overlap with Chart 2 and Chart 3.

1. R. Soposhna [River]

2. R. Icha [River]

3. R. Oblukovina [River]

4. R. Myshkuian [River]

5. R. Kutogorova [River]

6. R. Kompakova [River]

7. R. Vorovska [River]

8. R. Kol [River]

9. R. Nemtik [River]

10. R. Kikchik [River]

11. Utka [River]

12. Mytoga [River]

13. R. Bystra [River]

14. Bol'shaia [River]

15. Chekavka [River]

16. Ozerna [River]

NOTE: Nos. 13-16 form a single river system.

17. R. Apalai [River]

18. R. Golygina [River]

Chart 4

NOTE: Nos. 17 and 18 join near the mouth and debouch into the Okhotsk Sea through a single channel.

19. Koshegochik [River]

20. R. Ozerna [sic, River]

21. Kambalina [River]

22. Kuril'skaia Lopatka [Cape Lopatka, Kurile Lopatka]

23. Gavri [sic, Gavril, River]

24. Mutina [River]

25. Koshegochik [sic, same river name as under No. 19]

26. Viliunchik [River]

27. Paratunka [River]

28. Avacha [River]

29. Kalakhtyr' [River]

30. Nalacheva [River]

31. Ostrovna [River]

32. M. Shipunskoi [Cape]

33. M. Khaligerskoi [Cape]

34. R. Zhupanova [River]

35. R. Berezova [River]

36. M. Klin [Cape]

37. R. Shemiachik [River, cf. chart 2]

38. R. Kamyshki [River]

39. Kronok [River or/and lake]

40. R. Stolbova [River, cf. Charts 2 and Chart 3]

41. Stolbovoi [cape]

Chart 4

42. Kronotskoi [Cape]

43. Chazhma [River]

44. Chazhminskoi [Cape]

45. R. Kamchatka [Kamchatka River]

46. Kamchatskoi [Cape]

47. Avral [Cape]

48. Ozero Stolbovskoe [Lake]

49. Srtolbovoi [Cape]

NOTE: There is a Cape Stolbovoi, Stolbovskoe Lake and Stolbovaia River to the N of Kamchatka River and a river and cape of the same name to the S of Kamchatka River.

50. Alaid [Island]

51. 1st [Kurile Island], Soushum

52. 2nd [Kurile Island] Poromoshir

53. 3rd [Kurile Island] Shiriki [var. Shirinki]

54. 4th [Kurile Island] Mamrishi

55. 5th [Kurile Island] Onekotan

56. 6th [Kurile Island] Kharomikhotian

57. 7th [Kurile Island] Shniashkotan

58. 8th [Kurile Island] Chnarsha

59. 9th [Kurile Island] Chirenkotan

60. 10th [Kurile Island(s)] Eganta

61. 11th [Kurile Island] Rakoke

62. 12th [Kurile Island] Motoua

63. 13th [Kurile Island] Rashaua

Chart 4

64. 14th [Kurile Island] Ushir

65. 15th [Kurile Island] Ketoi

66. 16th [Kurile Island] Shiushar

CHART 5

Shows the continuation of the Kurile Island Chain, from the 16th through the 22nd island (Atkis), with only parts of the coastline of the 19th, 21st and 22nd islands represented. Lovtsov indicates Ainu settlements [Mokhnatskoe zhilishche], 13 on Itorba Island [Iturup], and a 14th settlement, apparently a Japanese outpost. On Kunashir, 6 Ainu villages are indicated. On Kunashir's southern shore is a harbor. On Atkis 4 Ainu villages are shown, as well as an anchorage of a Japanese vessel, and a Japanese barracks [kazarma iaponskaia].

North to south, the islands listed are as follows:

1. 15th [Kurile Island] Ketoi

2. 16th [Kurile Island] Shiushar

3. 17th [Kurile island] Chirpoi

4. Siuchei [unnumbered island, Sivuchii]

5. 18th [Kurile Island] Urup

6. 19th [Kurile] ostorv Itorba [only the W coast outlined]. Along the coastal line an inscription indicates "Mokhnatsoke zhilishche" [settlements of the Hairy Ainu]. Small circles, numbering ca. 59, indicate the locations of the settlements. An erupting volcano is drawn near the center of the Island.

7. 20th [Kurile Island] Kunashir. Four small circles near the E coast, six on the W coast, and ten along the S and SE coast indicate Ainu settlements. Two drawings of a fort, in association with the letter "K" indicate Japanese outposts. An erupting volcano is drawn near NE coast.

8. Inscription: "harbor mapped" indicates a bay on the S end of Kunashir.

9. 21st [Kurile island] Chikota. Only SW coast drawn, showing a coastal mountain range and an inland lake.

10. 22nd [Kurile Island] Atkis

11. Inscription stating "Mokhnatskoe zhilishche" [settlements of the Hairy Ainu] with 25 circles indicating the locations

Chart 5

12. A drawing of a fort and inscription "Kazarmy Eponskie" [Japanese barracks]

13. Inscription "Japanese vessel" (drawn in a bay near the Japanese fort)

CHART 6

Chart 6 is a very interesting map of Honshu Island, with the Korean coast designated as the "shore of the Island of Karan or Koreer." Within the cartouche, the inscription reads:

"Map of Japanese islands on which are indicated the land and sea routes used by the Dutchmen for the journeys from the City of Nagasaki to the City of Iedo where the king of these islands resides."

An unsigned typed statement, appended to the atlas, and probably made in the book dealership (Karl W. Hiersmann, Leipzig, from whom the atlas was acquired), suggests that this map is a copy of one made by the Jesuit Father Phillip de Briet in the 17th century. A comparison of the Lovtsov chart with that by de Briet, published in the Teleki atlas (1909) indicates that though the two maps are similar they are not identical. For example, as stated in the cartouche (the title), the sea and land routes from Nagasaki to the capital are indicated on Lovtsov's chart but not on de Briet's. Island Oki (Lovtsov, No. 34) is indicated as Orui by de Briet. In addition, Lovtsov's chart has a notation which is absent on de Briet's map:

"In the province of Imaisot, near the city of Ikaba, there are in the mountains very rich silver mines."

Therefore, we must conclude that while Lovtsov may have had in his possession Dutch charts and maps of Japanese islands, which he may have used as a base, it was not de Briet's map. Instead, the chart appears to be derived from the map by Durant-Tavernier which dates to 1679 (published by Teleki 1909). This derivation is established on the basis of conformity of general outlines of coastal features and the legends and travel routes indicated on both Durant-Tavernier and Lovtsov's charts. Both charts cover an area from $169°0"$ to $186°0"$ longitude and from $31°0'$ to $40°0'15"$ N latitude. However, Lovtsov's chart contains additional details.

Lovtsov's chart bears the following inscription within a cartouche:

"Chart of the Japanese Islands on which is indicated the route by sea and by land used by the Dutch when travelling from Nangasaki [sic] to the city of Iedo where resides the king of these islands".

[Karta ostrovov iaponskikh vneizhe oznachen put' kak morem tak sukhim putem egozhe gollantsy upotrebliaiut vproezde svoem isgrada nangasaki vgorod IEDO gde zhivet korol' onykh ostrovov].

This chart has 158 place names. The following inscriptions appear on Lovtsov's chart:

1. More Kioreer [The Sea of Korea]

Chart 6

2. Ostrov Karan ili Koreer [The island of Karan or Koreer, Korean coast]

Between the coast of Korea and Honshu, an unnamed relatively large island is shown (in addition to numerous small islets). Above this island, there is the following inscription which coincides with inscription on Durant-Tavernier chart:

"Ostrov vkotoroi vysylaiut molodykh detei koi nekhotiat rabotat' gde prinuzhdaiut rabotat' siloiu dotekh mest dondezhe idblizhnikh srodstevennik kto ikh vozmet" [An island to which are sent those young children who do not want to work where they are made to work by force until such place [sic] when one of their close relatives accepts them].

3. Firando, pervoe zhilishche gollantsov [Firando, the first abode of the Dutch, an off-shore island]

4. Ostrov i gorody Gato [var. Goto or Guto, Island and towns of Gato]

5. Kisma, ostrov gde nyne gollantsy [Kisma, island where the Dutch are now]

6. Uima [Tsima or Tsimo] Sankok, an off-shore island

7. Satkuma

8. More Iuzhnoe [The Southern Sea]

9. Tanebatsima [an off shore island]

10. Island on which Nagasaki is located, marked in the center: Khomo korolevstov Sankok [Khomo Sankok Kingdom]

11. Nangasaki, indicated by drawing of a large castle

11a. Legend pertaining to a bay on S shore of Khome, near Nagasaki: "V sie mesto priezhaiut korabli dlia vygruzki" [To this locality come ships to unload].

Along the shore, to WNW of Nagasaki, six small localities indicated by circles, as follows:

12. Dokan' [var. Dokani]

13. Zeta

14. Gama

Chart 6

15. Kanasti

16. Omodaki

17. Sikubi

Along the northern shore from W to E:

18. Aiva

19. Gobeno

20. Komai

21. Ganomiraki

22. Korora

23. Kokura

24. Legend reads: "Bige zhilishche 2 sshkami"

25. Fumai

26. Bunzhi

27. Vasumi

28. Ostrov Toko ezi ili Tsikoko [Island Tokoezi or Tsikoko]

29. Sanuan

30. Anan

31. Aka

32. Tsikoko

33. Tsiogio [Tsnogio]

34. Toia

35. Dongo or Dengo

36. Oki [Town or island off N shore]

Chart 6

37. Sadi [Town or Island off N shore. Legend reads: "Srebrena ruda" [Silver ore].

38. Tondo tsima [a group of 7 islands, off NW shore]

39. Proliv Sukgar [Sukgar Strait]

40. Zemlia Esso [Land of Esso, Hokkaido coast]

41. Mankuksima [Island off W coast]

42. Tou [Island off W coast, to the S of 41]

43. Tsimotsima [Island off W coast, to the S of 42]

In large lettering, four provinces or major regions are indicated, marked on xerox 42-44, omitted in the new numbering system:

Imansot [Western region]

Netsegem [central]

Kanto [northern]

Okhnor [southeastern]

44. Nanbato [NW extremity, city]

45. Tsimotsiri

46. Takomisaki

47. Rotoiauma

48. Iamangedu

49. Akri

50. Firo

51. Tokovari. Legend: "Sol'variat" [salt is boiled here]

52. Tsima

53. Tomo

54. Mikari

55. Idakuiro

56. Bingfa

57. Okaimo

58. Muro

59. Bingo

60. Bigu

61. Adzumo

62. Noama [Koama?]

On the peninsula, above the city #62, Noama, among a mountain range, the legend: "Zolota ruda" [Gold ore].

63. Foki

64. Iazuki

65. Mimalasa

66. Farima

67. Ikabo [city; above, off N shore the legend reads: In the province Iamansot, near the city of Ikaba, in the mountains, are most plentiful silver mineworks --- V provintsii Iamansot bliz' goroda Ikaba imeetsia v gorakh preizobil'neshiia srebrennye rudokopstva].

68. Totatori

69. Tauma

70. Tanbo

71. Tamba [?]

72. Tkunokuki

73. Miako ili Meako [large city]

74. Iakus

75. Fisiu

76. Akhias

77. Iamatsiro

78. Fukimi

79. Kakoza [Vakoza?]

80. Kviranets

81. Eshiten'

82. Komi

83. Antsuki

The above place names are for the western end of Honshu and around the inland lakes. The following set of place names are for the area E of the inland lakes, south of the town of Antsuki, and to the large river to the east flowing N to S.

84. Kvaio [?]

85. Oko

86. Tsoekast [tsoskast]

87. Omosudy avykha [anykho] dat' retenzi

88. Osoka

89. Bashnia

90. Sakana

91. Khedikma

92. Kvinokuni

93. Tsima [Uima?]

94. Iamataka

95. Sekino

96. Susanue [Susanus?]

97. Tsek [Uek?]

98. Innosue uo

99. Nanda

100. Ingo

101. Komvama [?]

102. Vaka

103. Evabs

104. Soki

105. Menakuta

106. Sinta

107. Ormida

From the extreme northern peninsula southward along the river:

108. Noto

109. Novma

110. Tsika

111. Kanga

112. Upshu

113. Kanatsaka

114. Fanda

115. Avaeari krukri

Inland towns off the river flowing NW:

116. Tsinamo

117. Kanzuk

118. Eshingo

119. Kivatas

Chart 6

120. Snova

121. Bash. [abbr. "tower"]

122. Tatanen [var. Tatanei]

123. Mikava

124. Mia gde delaiut lutchshie shpagi [Mia where the best swords are made].

125. Guiu

126. Iaka gde lutshii pol zhenskii [Iaka where the female gender is the best]

127. Kirak

128. Iaan

129. Biki

130. Barasakna [Barasia ?]

131. Fuzino ialinik [?] gora vsegda pokryta snegom [the mountain always covered with snow].

132. Bashnia [tower]

133. Skabarab [?]

134. Kivask

135. Bandel'

136. M. Misaki [Cape Misaki]

To NE of No. 135, "Bandel", the legend reads: V sei provintsii Kandy meetsia ruda srebrena [In this Province of Kanda there is silver ore].

137. Skvama

138. Lokna [?]

139. Sangaiam [? Sansami ?]

The following place names pertain to the area E of the N-S trail or province boundary, from S (peninsula) to NE along the coast:

140. Avi

141. Kanzula

142. Mulatsi

143. Tsimoli

144. Ansimot

145. Kiuk

146. Fitak

147. Satak

148. Kotsu

149. Tseidak zolotaia ruda [gold ore]

150. Liazu

151. Kokazav [?]

152. Kanbu

153. Gerigaita [? Gerigasta ?]

154. Lanta

CHART 7

This chart represents Anadyr' Bay. The main features are, from N to S as follows:

1. R. Nerpich'ia [River debouching into the Anadyr' Bay from N]

2. Anadyr' [River, lower course]

3. Ozero [A lake from which flows, from S, a tributary to the Anadyr']

4. R. Onemen' [River emptying into the inner bay of Anadyr' Bay from S]

5. G. Onemeiskaia [Onemei inlet, an inner bay of the Anadyr' Bay]

6. G. Bol'shaia [Bolshaia Bay, an inner bay of the Anadyr' Bay on the S].

7. Ugol Fadeiia [Fadei Corner, Cape]

8. R. Khatyrka [River]

9. Reka Opuka [River]

CHARTS 8a and 8b

This chart, compiled on the basis of descriptions available in Petropavlovsk archives which were submitted to Commander Behm by Cook's officers in 1779, shows Bering Strait. The chart comprises two pages. On the first page the chart shows the outline of Chukchi Peninsula [Chukotskii Nos, #1] and American Cape [Mys Amerikanskoi, #2]. Three islands are shown within the Strait itself, unnamed, two islands to SE of the Strait, presumably King and Sledge Islands, and two Islands SE of the Strait, presumably points of land on St. Lawrence Island.

At the top of the chart, a straight line (#4) is shown with part of the inscription (continued on the second page) "Po sei linii l'dy nepodvizhnyia" [along this line there was immovable ice].

The second page shows the continuation of the outline of the "American Cape" [#2] and the outline of the American coast to #3, "Bukhta Notrentseu" [Norton Sojend].

The outline of the American coast beyond the Bering Strait shows a break, and inscription within the cartouche reads:

"From lat. 68°0'00" to lat. 69°0'00" and longitude 219°30', fog and shallow water. Unable to sail [here] due to the shallowness of water".

CHART 9

This is a second chart Lovtsov compiled on the basis of data provided Commander Behm by Cook's officers. It shows, in rough outline, parts of the American coast of the Bering Sea from Bristol Bay to Norton Sound. Only the latter (#2) and "M. Niunem" [Cape Newenham] are named. The inscription within the cartouche reads:

"From latitude 60°00' to latitude 63°00', longitude 215°00' the shallowness of water made investigation impossible. The land, however, was visible throughout. What features there were, river or bay, is unknown."

CHART 10

This chart also may have been based on information provided by Cook's officers, possibly supplemented by data from earlier Russian naval expeditions available to Lovtsov in Petropavlovsk, notably data from Bering's second voyage and from the expedition under Krenitsyn and Levashev of 1768-1769. The chart shows the eastern Aleutians, the Alaska Peninsula and Bristol Bay to Cape Newenham, and on the Pacific side, islands from Kodiak to the Shumagins. Another note about fog and stormy weather precluding closer investigation is contained in a cartouche. Since by 1782 Kamchatka officers had a very good notion of the Aleutian Chain and Kodiak Island, this map was by then primitive.

The following features are indicated:

1. M. Niunem [Cape Newenham

2. Aliatsa [Alaska Peninsula]

3. Unimak Island

4. Krenitsyn Islands, unnamed, are indicated to SW of Unimak, followed by rough outline of the N and E shores of Unalaska Island (#4).

5. Ostrov Kad'iak [Kodiak Island, rough outline]

6. Ostrova Shumaginskiia [Shumagin Islands, 7 indicated in outline locations divergent from those on extant Bering expedition charts].

CHART 11

This is a rough outline of Kenai Peninsula, the "Great River" or "Cook's River" (now Cook Inlet), and part of Prince William Sound (called here, after Captain Cook, Sandwich Sound). It is clearly based on descriptions provided by Cook's Officers. Features are indicated as follows:

1. Grusa Flius [Grosses Fluss, German for Big River, or Cook's River, modern Cook Inlet]

2. M. Germogena [Cape Hermogen]

3. Zenvich Saun [Sandwich Sound, modern Prince William Sound]

CHART 12

Outline of a part of SW Alaska coast, part of Prince William Sound. Inscription within the cartouche, presumably based on data supplied by Cook's officers, reads:

"Bay 58°20', longitude 240°45'. How far it stretches it was impossible to ascertain because of shallowness of water."

Underneath, inscription apparently supplied by Lovtsov out of his own knowledge:

"Captain Commander Bering was at this coast on the 20th day of July in the year 1741."

CHART 13

A rough outline of the NW Coast of North America, two points marked, separated by a break:

1. L. America

2. Point marked by inscription:

"Captain Chirikov was at this coast on the 15th day of July in the year 1741."

Inscription within the cartouche, presumably derived from the notes compiled on the basis of information supplied to Commander Behm by Cook's officers, reads:

"From the latitude 50°07' to latitude 55°23', and from longitude 249°30' to longitude 243°50' the land could not be seen because of fog and storms."

CHART 14

This is apparently the last chart constructed on the basis of information supplied to Kamchatka authorities by Cook's officers. It shows a rough outline of the coast of North America roughly from lat. 43° to 49° (with breaks). These charts are rather primitive, and we can only suppose that if Cook's officers did leave charts of their voyage with Governor Behm (and if these charts stayed in Kamchatka after Behm's departure), they were schematic representations made for the purpose, not exact copies of charts compiled by Cook's excellent cartographers on the voyage. However, we know that Behm, when leaving Kamchatka, took with him several charts from Cook's expedition, of which most if not all were then taken from him in Irkutsk in the Governor's office (anonymous a and b). Five charts (two of them rare variants) which may be connected with Cook's expedition have been located in the Navy Archives of the USSR in Leningrad, and were examined by A.C.F. David (RN, ret.). Of these, two are composites, compiled in 1780 and 1781 on which Cook's discoveries are indicated. The chart dated 1780 shows, in an inset, the plan of Avatcha, similar to that which appears in Lovtsov's atlas (see below, Chart 18). The named points are:

1. (Northernmost point): L. America

2. Vinzhor Sound [Windsor Sound]

3. Novyi Albion [New Albion]

The inscription within the cartouche reads:

"From the latitude 45°00' to latitude 47°00', longitude 253°30' the land could not be seen because of fog and storms. Unknown if a bay or something else."

CHART 15a and 15b

This chart consists of two pages and is a composite chart of the Aleutian Islands. It shows part of the Kamchatka coast and islands of the Aleutian chain, some unnamed. The island names which appear on the chart suggest that Lovtsov used for background data provided by Bering's second expedition of 1741 and Chirikov's sail to the Near Islands in 1742, with additional information from the Krenitsyn-Levashev expedition, as well as data on the Commander Islands supplied by merchant skippers after 1745.

Page 1 shows Kamchatka coast, Commander Islands, and westernmost Aleutians as follows:

1. M. Stolbovskoi [Cape]

2. O. Stolbovskoe [Lake]

3. Avral [Cape]

4. M. Chazhminskoi [Cape]

5. Chazhma [River]

6. M. Kronotskoi [Cape]

7. R. Stolbova [River]

8. Stolbovskoi [2d cape of that name]

9. M. Klin [Cape]

10. Berezova [River]

11. M. Khaligerskoi [Cape]

12. Zhupanova [River]

13. Ostrov Beringov [Bering Island]

14. Ostrov Mednoi [Mednoi or Copper Island]

15. Ostrova Obmanchivyia [the Deception Islands, Obmanchivyia]

16. Ostrov S. Avramiia [St. Avraam island]

One island shown is unnamed.

Page 2 shows several islands of the Aleutian Chain named by Bering in 1741:

17. Ostrov Sv. Fedora [Amchitka?]

18. Ostrov Sv. Stefana

An unnamed island is shown to the E of #18.

19. Ostrov Sv. Makariia.

Three unnamed islands and the outline of the western extremity of the fourth are shown to the E of #19.

CHART 16

The sources for this chart of the eastern Aleutians cannot be ascertained. It is apparently based on Bering and Chirikov's expedtion of 1741, with additional information from the Krenitsyn-Levashev expeditions. The chart shows some of the Andreanof Islands of the Aleutian Chain, the Four Mountains Islands, and the Fox Islands to the tip of Alaska Peninsula, with partial outline of Kodiak Island. The chart is extremely crude and does not conform to the much more detailed and sophisticated charts of the Aleutian Chain compiled by various merchant skippers prior to 1782. The place names also are grossly distorted. They read as follows:

1. Sekulan [presumably referring to Seguam, though the location and outline do not conform to the state of the art]

2. Kagamom [presumably refers to Kagamil, but the outline and location do not conform to the state of the art]

3. Umnak [incorrectly represented as a group of four small islets]

4. Unalashka [Unalaska Island drawn in crude outline, the same as on Chart 10]

5. Umnak [sic, indicating Unimak island]

6. Aliatsa [Alaska Peninsula]

7. Kad'iak [Kodiak Island]

CHART 17

This is a chart of the Shumagin Islands and Kodiak. As with Chart 16 it is not clear what documents were used by Lovtsov in compiling these charts, but it also is apparently based on the Bering-Chirikov expedition of 1741 and additonal information from the Krenitsyn-Levashev expeditions.

CHART 18

The last chart is a copy of the Cook expedition's chart of Petropavlovsk Harbor. Comparison with other charts of Petropavlovsk in the British archives suggests that this chart is based on one by Roberts, with Lovtsov interpolating his own knowledge of the harbor, adding additional soundings and correcting several place names to the Russian names used customarily. (See David, 1990.)

This chart is entitled in Russian, within the cartouche at top right "Plan of the S. Paul and Peter harbor with depth and shoal measurements." [Plan S. Petropavloskoi gavani s promerom glubiny i banok, sic]. On the left top there is a copied English inscription: "Pl. AN. of. the. BAY. of AWATSCHA. 1779" [sic]. At the bottom left, within a cartouche, scale, with an inscription underneath "sc ate of Miles" [sic]. It is, then, clear that this chart is based on one compiled by a member of Cook's Third Voyage. The authorship of the Cook's Voyage chart cannot be established with certainty, but it is likely to have been drawn by Henry Roberts. This opinion is based on comparison of soundings (and density of soundings) on the chart from Robert's journal (Mitchell Library MS.Q152, p.m 119, photo courtesy Cdr. A.C.F. David). Place names on the Lovtsov chart, however, differ from those appearing in English on Robert's chart, as well as the outline of the NW section. Also, Roberts' chart indicates topographical features of the harbor's shores, lacking on Lovtsov's chart (for comparison see fig. 19, Roberts' chart; for fuller discussion of possible authorship of Cook's Voyage chart, see accompanying text).

The place names which appear on Lovtsov's chart are as follows:

1. R. Paratunka [Paratunke River]

2. Paratunskoi ostrog [Paratunskoi fort] and small conventional drawing indicating Russian settlement.

3. G. Tareinskaia [Tareinskaia Inlet or Bay]

4. G. Rakova [Rakova Inlet or Bay]

5. S. Petropavlovskaia Gavan' [Petropavlovsk Harbor].

Chart 1

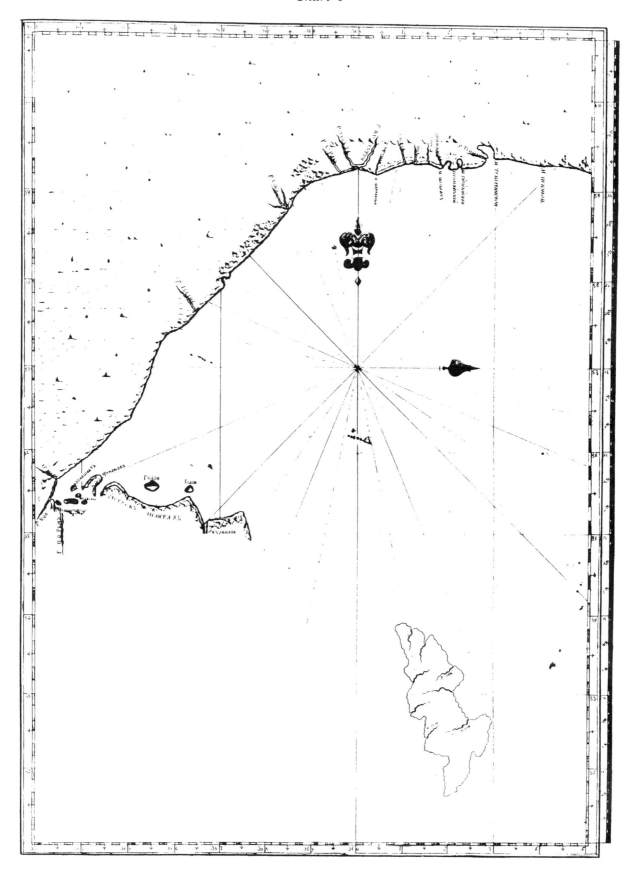

Chart 2

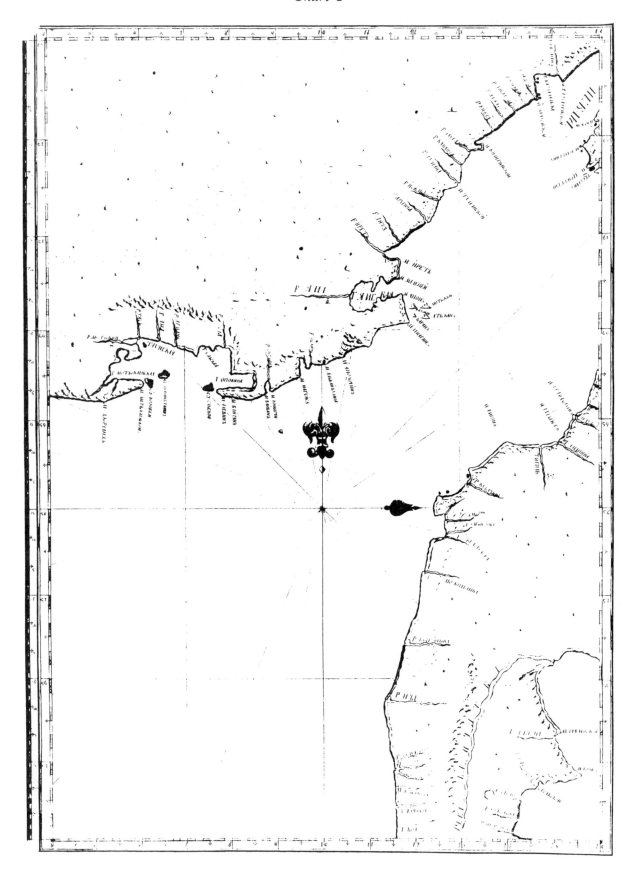

Chart 3

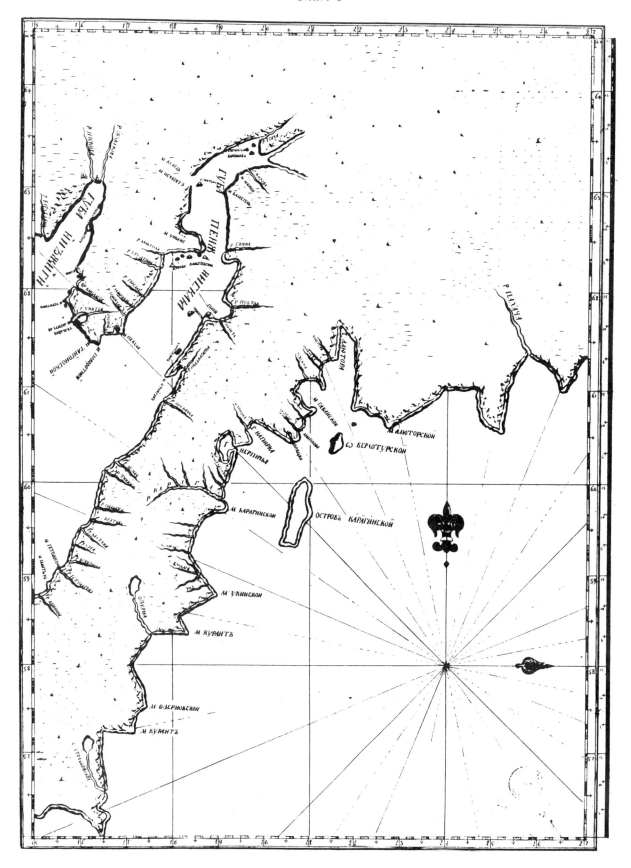

Chart 4

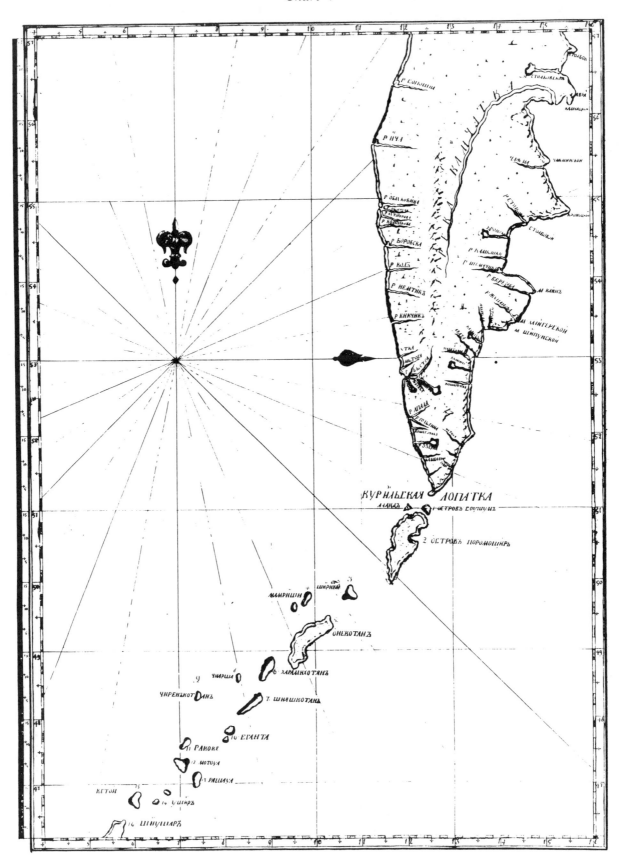

Chart 5

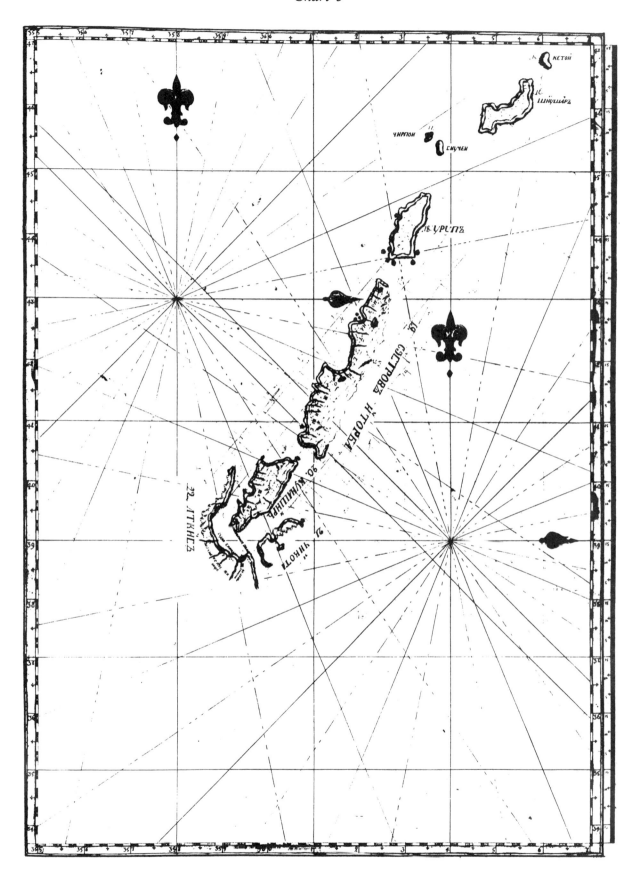

Chart 6

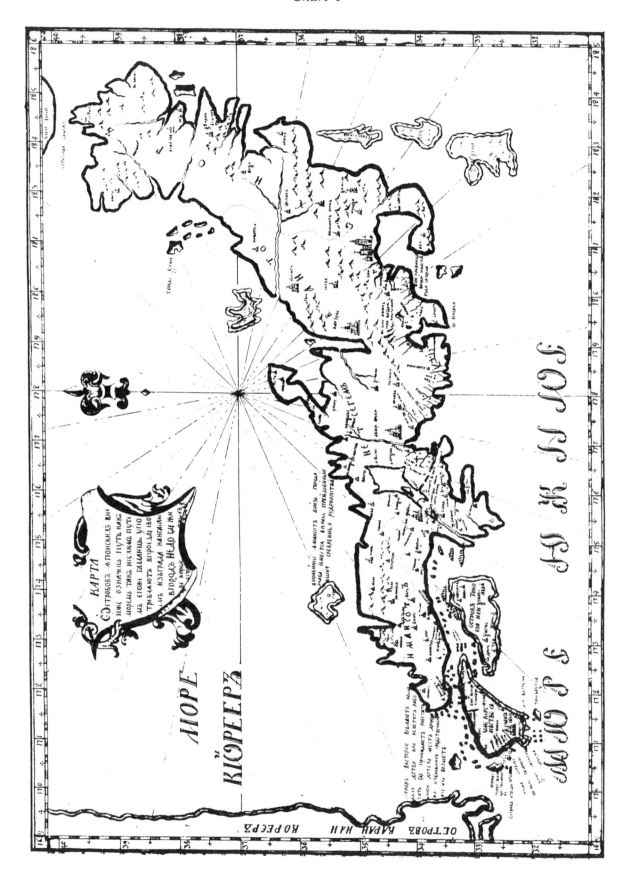

Chart 7

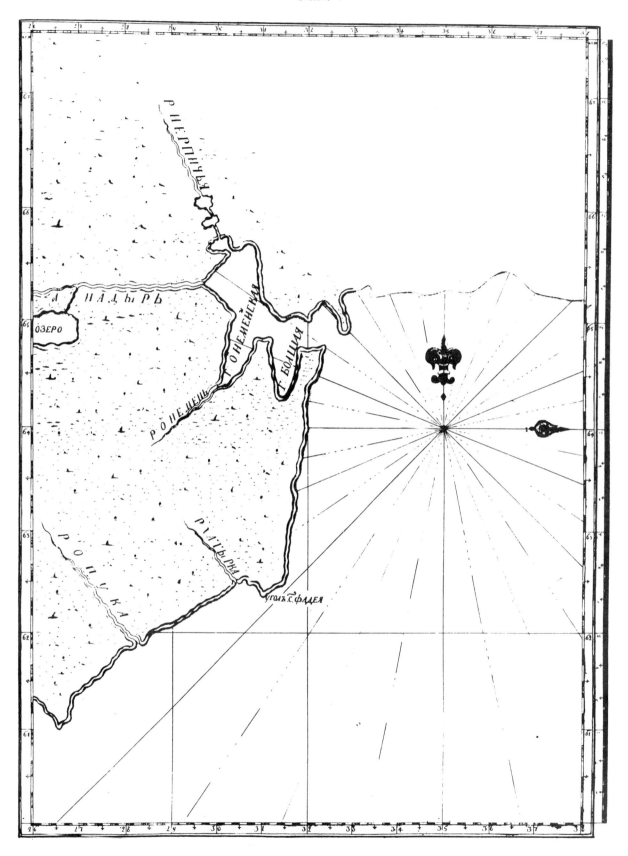

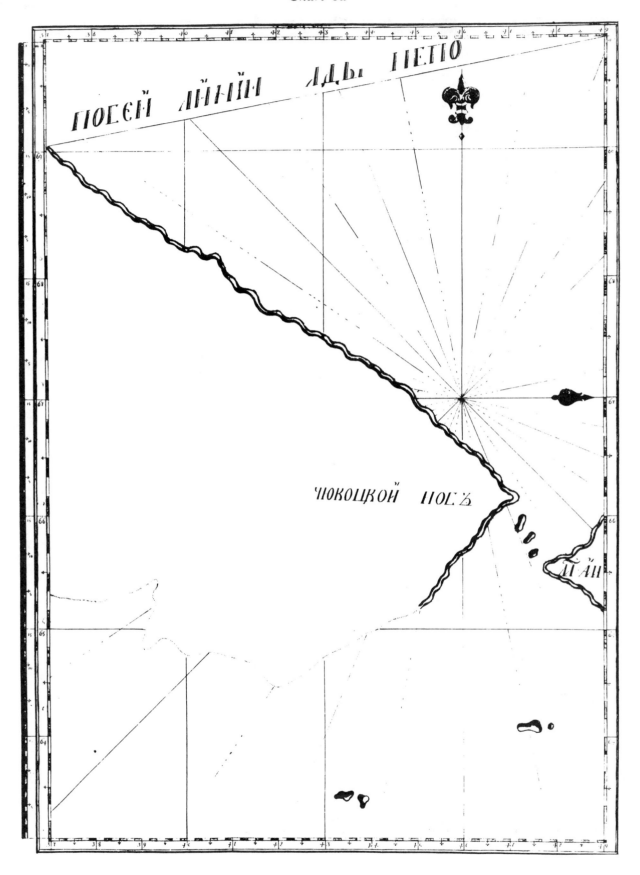

48

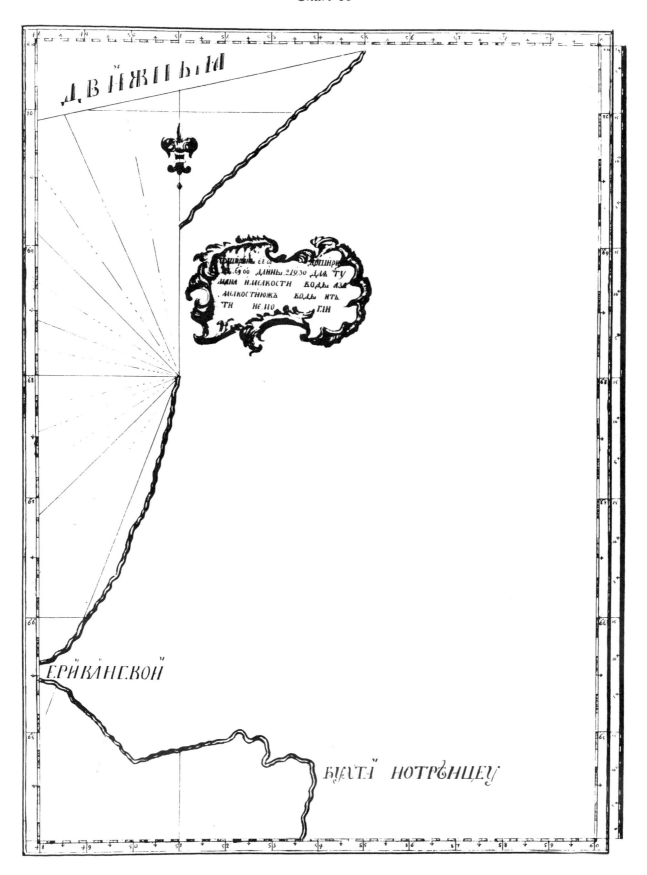

Chart 9

Chart 10

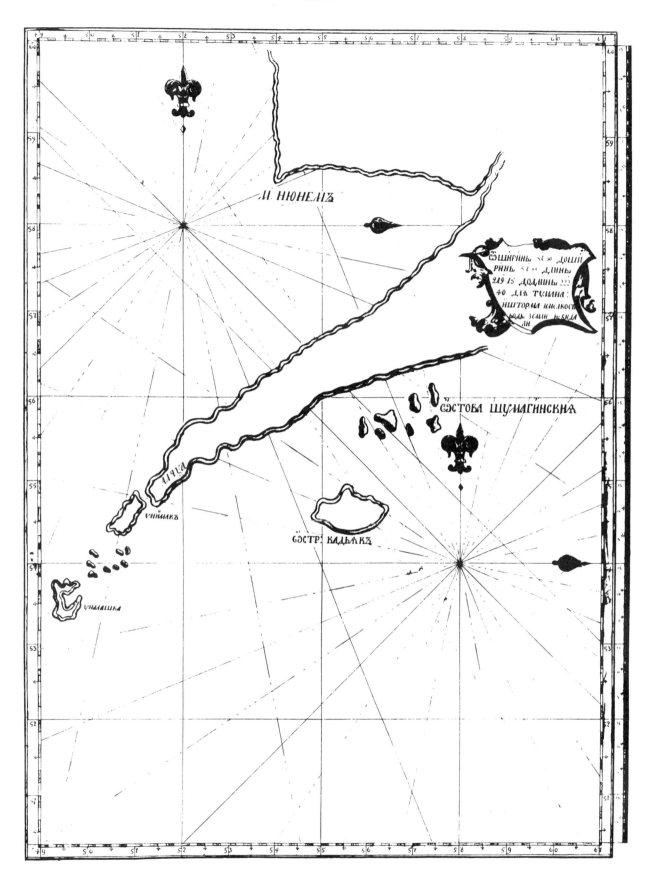

Chart 11

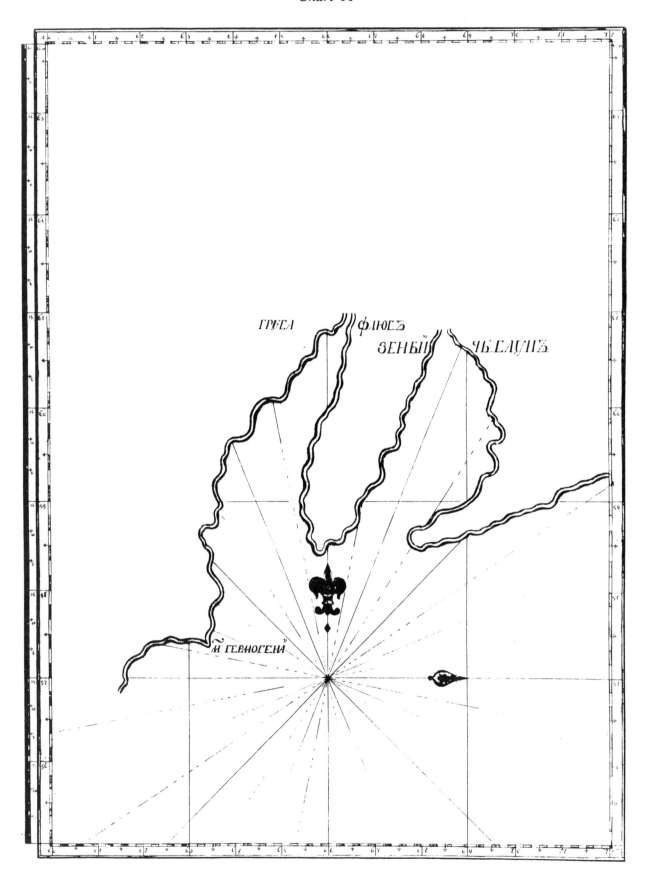

Chart 12

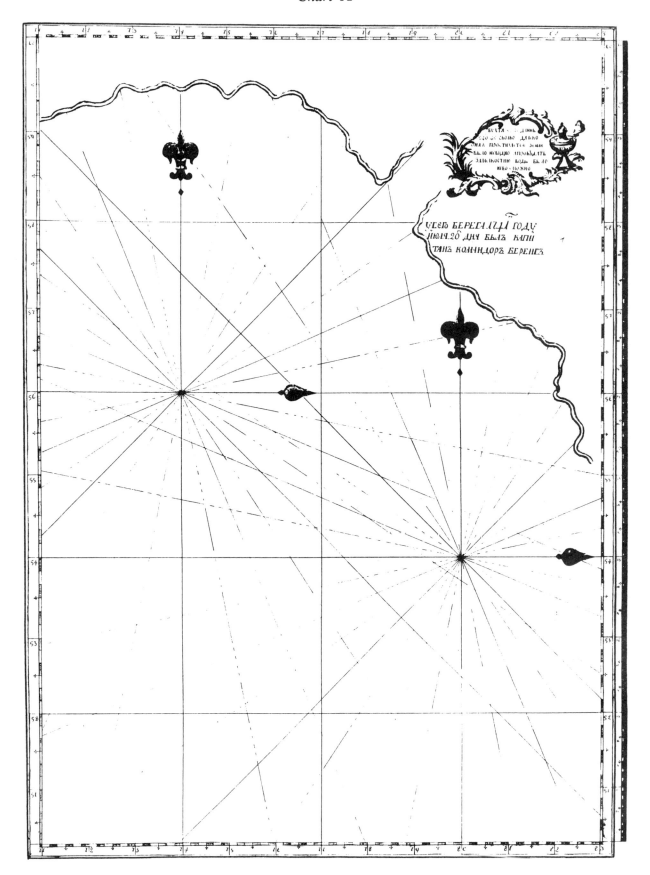

Chart 13

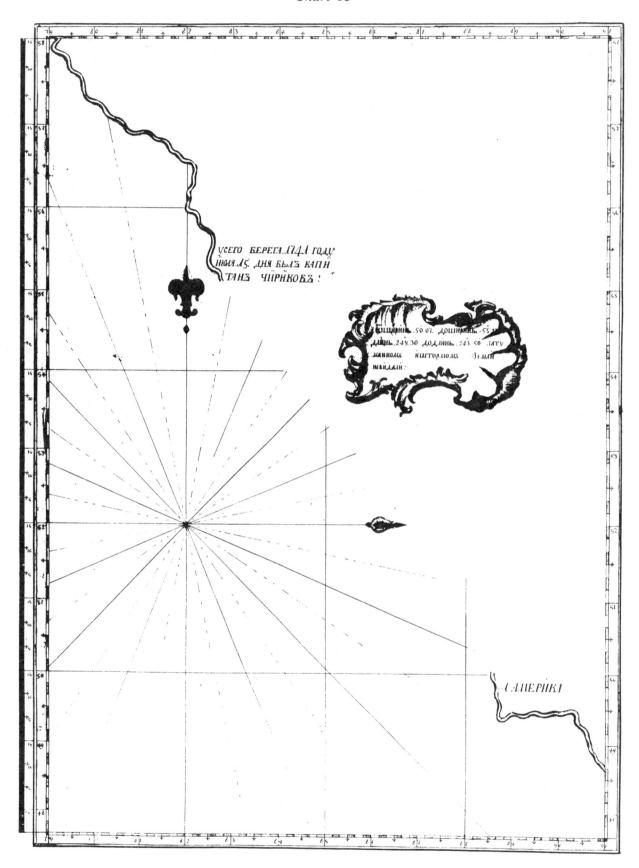

УСЕГО БЕРЕГА 1741 ГОДУ
ИЮНЯ 15 ДНЯ БЫЛЪ КАПИ
ТАНЪ ЧИРИКОВЪ :

КОШИРИНЬ 50 07 ДОШИРИНЬ 55
ДЛИНЬ 249 30 ДОДЛИНЬ 243 50 ЗАТУ
МАННОМЪ ИНШТОРИЛОМЪ ЗЕМЛИ
НЕВИДАЛИ :

САМЕРИКА

Chart 14

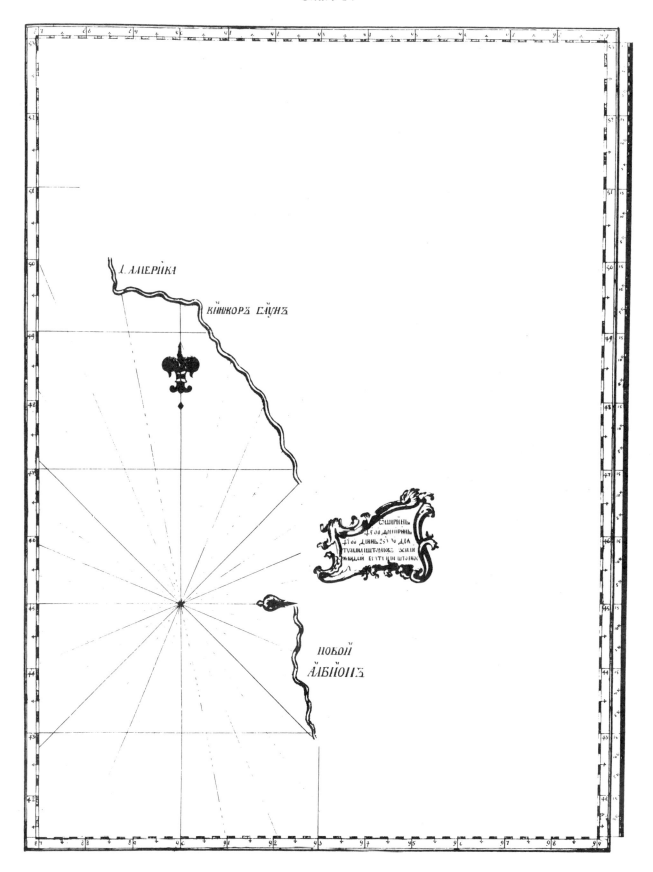

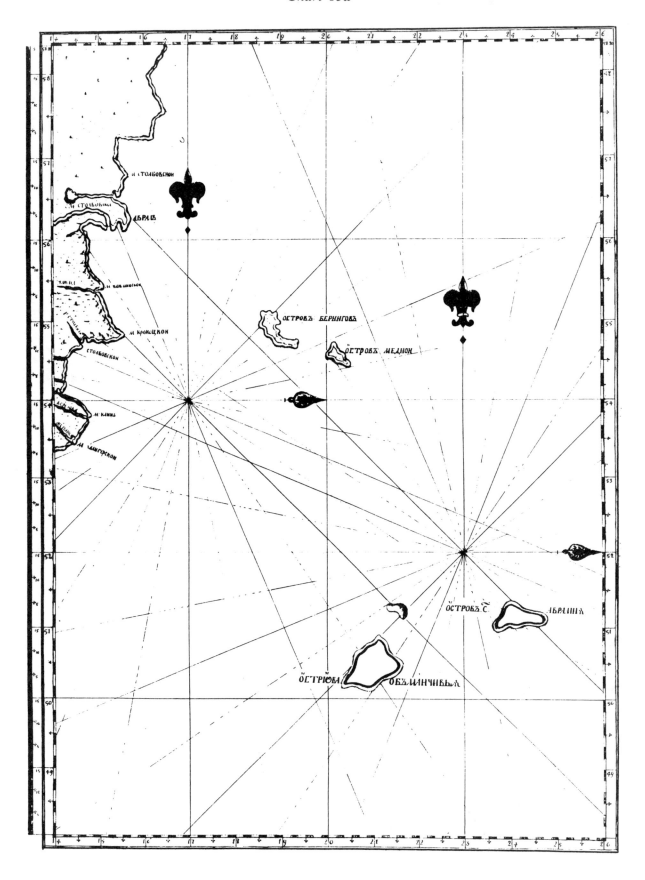

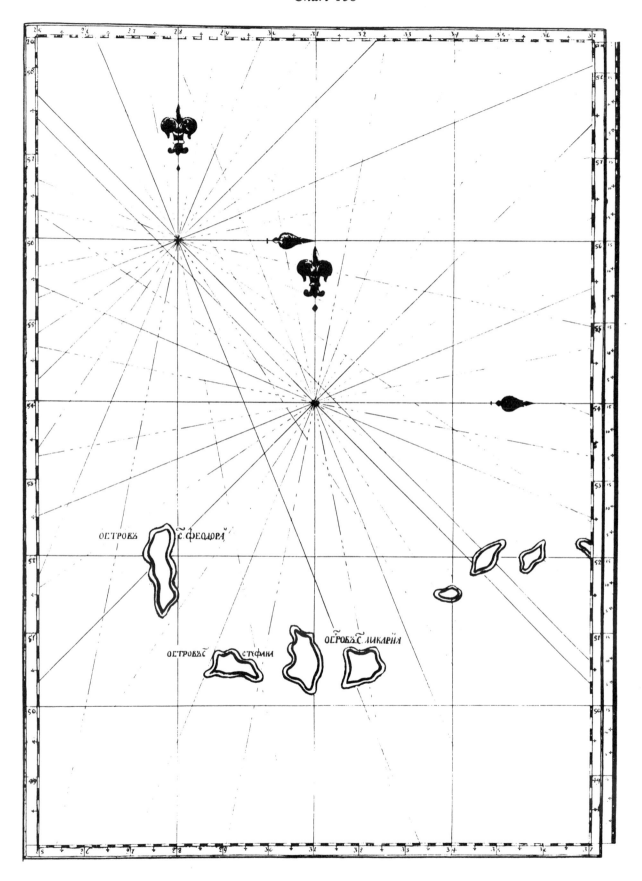

ОСТРОВЪ С. ѲЕОДОРА

ОСТРОВЪ С. СТѲѲАНА

ОСТРОВЪ С. МАКАРІА

57

Chart 17

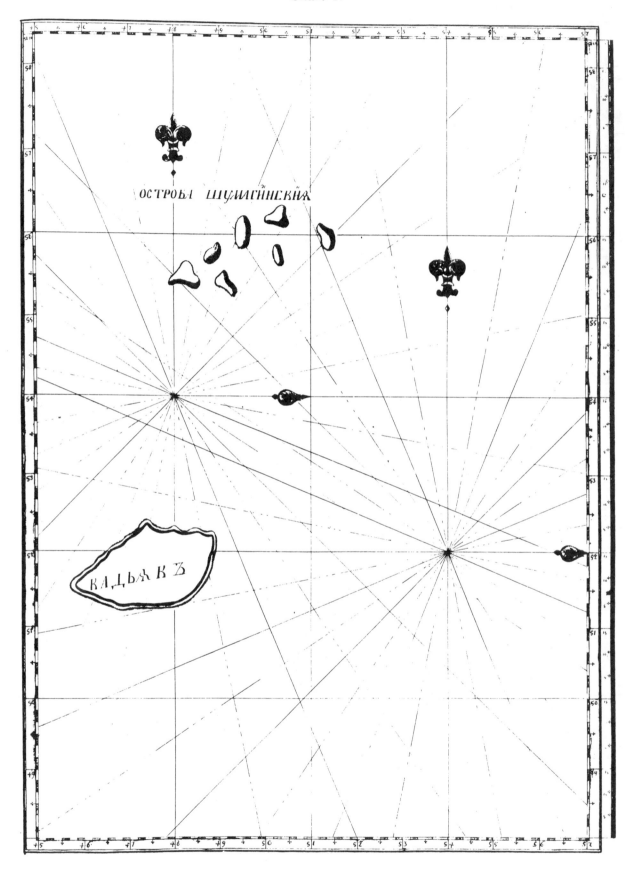

ОСТРОВА ШУМАГИНСКИЯ

КАДЬЯКЪ

Chart 16

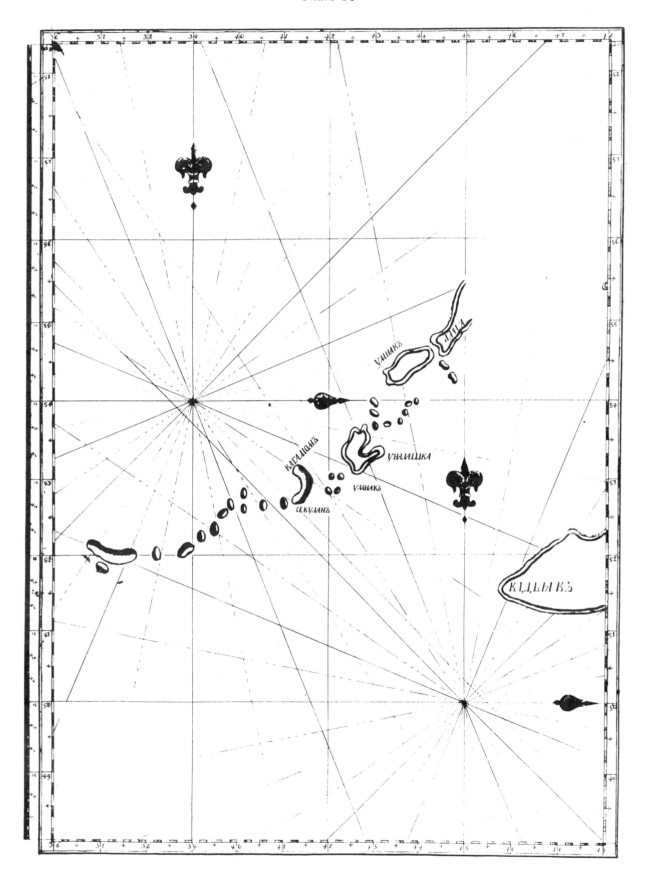

Chart 18

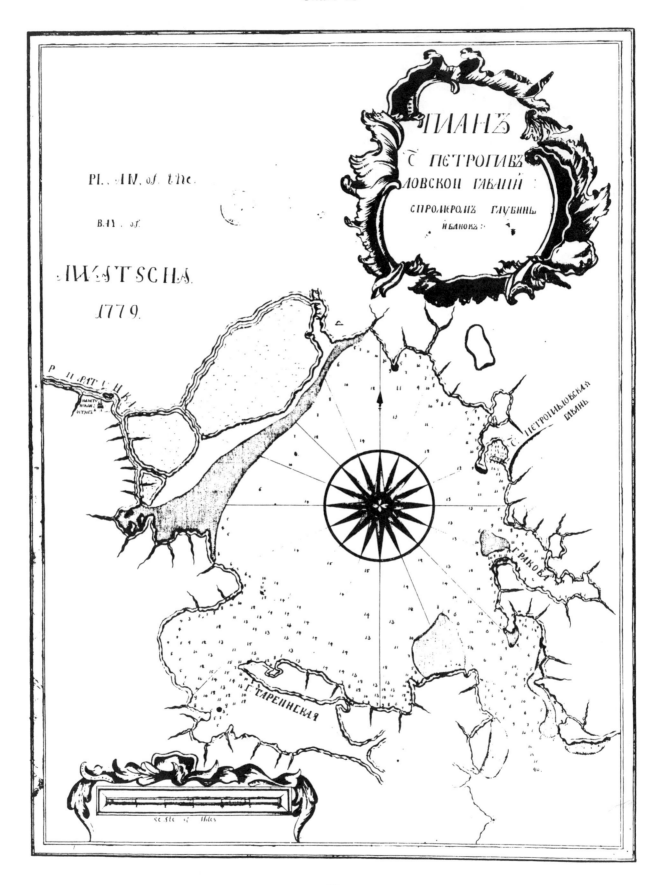

REFERENCES

Alekseev, A.I., Okhotsk-kolybel' Russkogo Tikhookeanskogo Flota, Khabarovsk, 1958.

Beregovaia Cherta. Magadan, 1987.

Anonymous, Magnus Karl von Bem, Sibirskii Vestnik, 21, Part 1, Book 5, St. Petersburg, 1823, pp. 1-14.

Anonymous, Vazhneishiia obstoiatel'stva zhizni i sluzhby byvshago Kamchatskago nachal'nika Bema (based on Bem's statement, 1781). Severnyi Arkhiv, vol. 13, 1827, Part III, "Biography," pp. 33-47.

Bagrow, Leo, A History of Russian cartography up to 1800. 2 vols., Henry W. Castner, editor, Wolfe Island, Ontario: The Walker Press, 1975.

Beaglehole, J.C., Cook and the Russians: an addendum to the Hakluyt Society's edition of "The Voyage of the Resolution and Discovery, 1776-1780." London, British Museum, The Hakluyt Society, 1973.

David, Andrew, Russian Charts and Captain Cook's Third Voyage, The Map Collector, 52:2-7.

Divin, V.A., Russkie moreplavaniia na Tikhom okeane v XVIII veke. Moscow, Mysl', 1971.

Divin, V.A., compiler and editor, Russkaia tikhookeanskaia epopeia. Khabarovsk, 1979.

Friss, Herman R., editor, The Pacific Basin: A history of its geographic exploration. New York, American Geographical Society, Special Publication #38, 1967.

Kopylov, A.N., Ocherki kul'turnoi zhizni Sibiri XVII - nachala XIXV. Novosibirsk: Nauka, 1974.

Lensen, George A., Report from Hokkaido: the remains of Russian culture in northern Japan. Westport, Connecticut. Greenwood Press, 1973. Originally published 1954 by the Municipal Library of Hakodate, Hakodate, Japan.

Lupach, V.C. editor, Russkie moreplavateli. Moscow: Voennoe Izdatel'stvo, Ministry of Defense, USSR, 1953.

Medushevskaia, O.M., Kartograficheskie istochniki po istorii russkikh geograficheskikh otkrytii na Tikhom okeane vo vtoroi polovine XVIII v., 1954.

Trudy Moskovskogo gosudarstvennogo istoriko-archivnogo instututa, V. 7. English translation by James R. Gibson 1972 in <u>The Canadian Cartographer</u>, 9:99-121 (December 1972).

See also <u>Essays on the History of Russian Cartography 16th to 19th Centuries</u>. Selected and translated by James R. Gibson, introduction by Henry W. Castner. Toronto, Canada, University of Toronto Press.

Polonskii, A., <u>Kurily</u>. <u>Zapiski Russkago Geograficheskago Obshchestva po otdeleniu etnografii</u>, St. Petersburg, 1871.

Raskin, N.M. and I.I. Shafronovskii, <u>Erik Gustafovich Laksman, vydaiushchiisia puteshestvennik i naturalist XVIII v.</u>, Leningrad, 1971.

Sauer, Martin, <u>An Account of a Geographical and Astronomical Expedition to the Northern Parts of Russia</u>, London, 1802.

Sgibnev, A.S., Okhotskii port. <u>Morskoi Sbornik</u> #11, 1869.

Shibanov, F.A., <u>Studies in the history of Russian cartography</u>, Parts 1 & 2, Cartographic Monographs #14 & #15. Toronto, Canada, University of Toronto Press, 1975.

Skelton, R.A., editor, <u>The Journals of Captain James Cook on his voyages of discovery</u>. Charts and views drawn by Cook and his officers and reproduced from the original manuscripts. Cambridge, The University Press, 1955.

Svet, Ia. M., Novye dannye o prebyvanii na Kamchatke Tret'ei ekspeditisii Dzh. Kuka (1779). In <u>Novoe v izuchenii Avstralii i Okeanii</u>, pp. 219-227. K.V. Mikhailovskii, editor. Moscow, Nauka, 1972.

Wagner, Henry R., <u>Cartography of the Northwest Coast of America to the Year 1800</u>. 2 vols. Berkeley, California, University of California Press, 1937.

Teleki, Paul, <u>Atlas der Geschichte der Kartographie der Japanischer Inseln</u>. Budapest and Leipzig, 1909.